MOST OF ALL

Story by Joanne Hyunjoo Lee

Pictures by Elizabeth Suh

Most of All

To Joshua and Sharon

MOST OF ALL

Story by Joanne Hyunjoo Lee   Pictures by Elizabeth Suh

I have many things.
I do!

I have a cat
that goes into my hat.

But I don't have a cap that goes with my bat.

I have a raincoat that matches my boots.

But I don't have shoes that match my suit.

I have a sack
hanging on my back.

But I don't have a lunch box to carry
my snack.

I have a robot to pull my toy truck.

But I don't have a tub to float my rubber ducks.

I have a spining top fast and strong.

But I don't have a jump rope shiny and long.

I have a pouch to keep
my marbles.

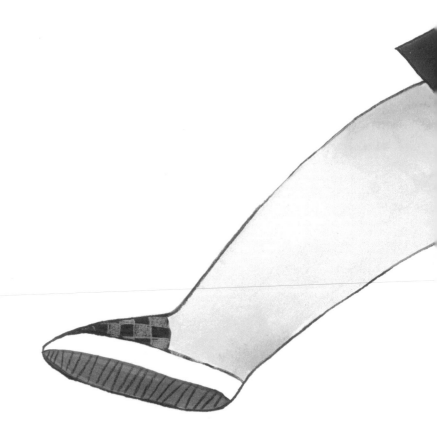

But I don't have a stick to make some bubbles.

I have a spade to build my castle.

But I don't have a candy to blow some whistles.

I have many things.
I really do!

cat

boots

sack

robot

top

pouch

spade

But...

There she comes!
My favorite one indeed!

She is my mom,
And that's ALL I NEED!

As for me, I shall behold your face in righteousness;
when I awake, I shall be satisfied with your likeness.
Psalms 17:15 ESV

WestBow Press books may be ordered through booksellers or by contacting:

WestBow Press
A Division of Thomas Nelson & Zondervan
1663 Liberty Drive
Bloomington, IN 47403
www.westbowpress.com
844-714-3454

Because of the dynamic nature of the Internet, any web addresses or links contained in this book may have changed since publication and may no longer be valid. The views expressed in this work are solely those of the author and do not necessarily reflect the views of the publisher, and the publisher hereby disclaims any responsibility for them.

Any people depicted in stock imagery provided by Getty Images are models, and such images are being used for illustrative purposes only.
Certain stock imagery © Getty Images.

Interior Image Credit: Elizabeth Suh

ISBN: 978-1-6642-0760-8 (sc)
ISBN: 978-1-6642-0761-5 (e)

Library of Congress Control Number: 2020919094

Print information available on the last page.

WestBow Press rev. date: 10/05/2020

WESTBOW
PRESS®
A DIVISION OF THOMAS NELSON
& ZONDERVAN